Native American Legends

- Builds Fluency
- Comprehension Checks
- 7 Reproducible Scripts
- Additional Fluency Passages
- Before and After Activities
- Listening Skills Worksheets
- Cross-Curricular Script Content and Activities

I0155014

Readers Theater
Fluency and Comprehension

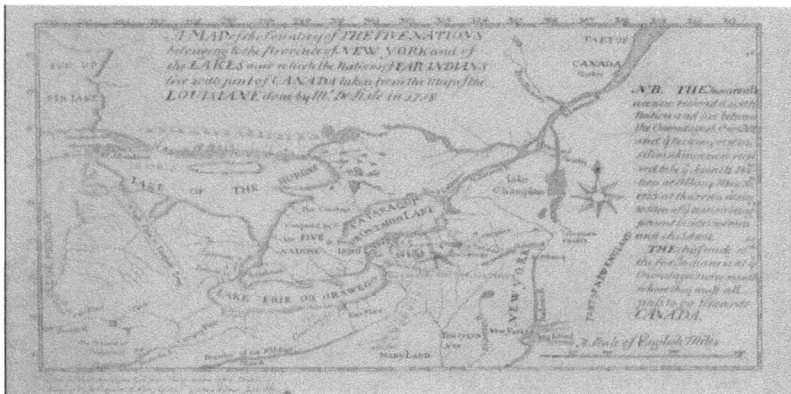

Grades 3-6

ISBN: 978-1-7323301-5-3

Publisher's Note: This book was made by humans -- if you find errors or typos – please let us know and they will be immediately researched and, if appropriate, fixed.

Borders are © Krista Wallden and may be found for purchase at: http://www.teacherspayteachers.com/store/Krista-Wallden

Table of Contents

Name: _____

1. Which readers theater did you participate in? _____
_____

2. What character did you play? _____

3.. List three character traits you have that are similar to the character you played:

_____   _____   _____

4. List three character traits you have that differ from the character you played:

_____   _____   _____

Directions: Summarize the readers theater skit you participated in:

_____
_____
_____
_____
_____
_____
_____
_____
_____
_____
_____
_____
_____
_____
_____
_____

Choose your favorite character from any of the Native American Legends readers theater scripts and explain why it is your favorite.

Favorite Character: _____

_____
_____
_____
_____
_____
_____
_____
_____
_____
_____
_____
_____
_____
_____

RL.3 – Comparing Versions

1. Compare the characters in the two versions of "The Fire Thief" readers theaters scripts. How are they similar? How are they the different?

_____
_____
_____
_____
_____
_____
_____
_____
_____
_____

2. Describe the settings from "The Fire Thief" readers theater scripts. How are they the same? _____

_____
_____
_____
_____
_____
_____

3. How are they different? _____

_____
_____
_____
_____

Close Reading Non-Fiction

1. **First Reading:** "Read to understand"
   a) Just reading
   b) No writing
   c) Getting an overview of the jest of a piece

2. **Second Reading:** "Read for details"
   a) Underline
   b) Make connections, annotate
   c) Think and question

3. **Third Reading:** "Read for purpose"
   a) Use details
   b) Gain a deeper understanding of text
   c) Make inferences
   d) Analyze, gather evidence from text

Readers Theater
Fluency and Comprehension

THE THEFT OF FIRE - VERSION 1

A Miwok Myth Adapted from Stories by Thomas Williams (1917)

CCSSRI: Read closely to determine what the text says explicitly and to make logical inferences from it; cite specific textual evidence when writing or speaking to support conclusions drawn from the text.

The theft of fire for the benefit of humanity is a myth, or legend, found in many cultures – from African to Ancient Greece to First Nations to Shoshone to Miwok, to many others. The common theme is that by stealing, or finding, fire - civilization advanced. In some myths, civilization advanced for the good. In others, the discovery of fire tore people apart – as in "The Theft of Fire" readers theater based on the Miwok legend.

"The Theft of Fire" adaptation by Thomas Williams is the legend that inspired version one's readers theater script. The legend was put to paper in a collection of Miwok Myths published in 1917 by Edward Winslow Gifford. Gifford used transcripts of Williams reciting "The Theft of Fire" , and other, legends in traditional oral fashion. Gifford was careful to write the stories exactly as they were spoken.

Native American legends, including "The Theft of Fire", used to be told at night in the circular assembly houses of the Miwok. They were recited by select men who traveled from village to village. Each storyteller was paid for their services. Payment came in the form of baskets, beads, furs and food. Many of the legends were chanted.

Each legend, whether told or chanted, was accompanied by songs of the various characters. The theft of fire is a universal tale. Have you ever heard it before?

Third Read Questions

The main idea of the article is: _____

_____

Write two details that support the main idea:

1. _____

_____

2._____

_____

Miwok Roundhouse Warm-Up

These photographs are of the Chaw Se' Roundhouse at Indian Grinding Rock State Park in Volcano, California. This is a working roundhouse for local Miwok and is similar to the ones that appear in "The Theft of Fire" readers theater scripts. In the legends; however, they are referred to as "assembly halls."

The plaque outside this roundhouse reads: "Our Sacred Space – A Miwok Roundhouse: the Hun'ge." The plaque furthers to inform park goers that only a tribal headsman could and can construct a hun'ge – as to do so is a great responsibility.

Why? Because roundhouses were, and still are, the center of community life for the Miwok. Every element of the structure has spiritual significance. When a headsman dies, the hun'ge he created is destroyed or abandoned.

The roundhouse at Chaw Se' is a functioning roundhouse. Additionally, it stands as a powerful symbol of cultural survival. Despite the tragic loss of life and land suffered by the Native community members - the roundhouse is a living testament to their strength and courage. This roundhouse is used year round. In Volcano, it is not uncommon to hear ancient chants and beating drums float through the air well into the night.

What is the significance of the roundhouse at Chaw Se"?

_____
_____
_____
_____
_____
_____
_____
_____

Who builds a roundhouse and why?

_____
_____
_____
_____
_____
_____
_____
_____
_____

THE THEFT OF FIRE - VERSION 1

A Miwok Myth Adapted from Stories by Thomas Williams (1917) – 3.0 Reading Level

The Miwok people lived in the San Joaquin Valley and in the foothills of the Sierra | 16
Nevada Mountains. Long ago, the people who gathered in the roundhouse of the San | 30
Joaquin River had fire. Those who gathered at the assembly house, or roundhouse, of the | 45
Geese, had none. The roundhouse of the Geese was in present day Tuolumne County. | 59

The birds and animals and men were all one. Lizard laid on top of a large rock looking | 77
down at the great valley below. "They have fire in the valley," he said. | 91

Coyote happened by. "I don't see fire," he said -- following Lizard's eyes with his own. | 106
"See the sparks coming out of the top of the roundhouse?" Lizard asked. | 120
"I don't even see the roundhouse," Coyote answered. | 128

Lizard sometimes told tall tales, but his voice was different this time and Coyote | 134
believe what he said. Coyote went to the Geese Assembly. "Lizard says there is fire in | 136
the valley." | 147

"Lizard! Ha! That one there, he tells tales," Black Goose said. | 154

"Could you see it?" White Goose asked. | 170

Coyote told them he could not, but would go back at dusk when sparks would be | 189
easier to see. Lizard was still on the rock. This time Coyote saw the fire, then ran back to | 192
tell the others. | 207

The assembly decided to send Flute-player, with four flutes, down into the valley | 223
to gather some fire for their people. Flute-player hurried down into the valley, but when | 239
he got to the roundhouse, by the great San Joaquin River, the door was blocked. Bear, | 254
Mountain Lion and Rattlesnake guarded it well. He decided to try the smoke hole, but | 269
Eagle blocked the opening with the span of one large wing. Only Eagle was asleep. | 284

Flute-player thought and thought about how to get in. Finally, he took out his blade | 294
and cut off two of Eagle's feathers and slipped inside. He found everyone sleeping, so | 308
he put fire in his four flutes and slipped away. | 321

People inside the assembly house began to stir. Little Bear saw Flute-player running | 336
towards the hills. "It's Flute-player and he's stolen some of our fire." | 354

The valley assembly summoned Wind, Rain and Hail to go after him. Hail caught up | 371
with him first. Flute-player hid his flutes in the river and convinced Hail he had no fire. | 375

Flute-player arrived home with the fire and started to pass it out. He began in the | 390
center and went outward. | 391

Coyote was farthest away and was cold, so he called to Flute-player, "Give some | 406
here." | 421

Flute-player blew the last of his coals to Coyote. Then things became confused. The | 422
Great Spirit was angry with Coyote and the people, so he made them speak different | 439
languages. | 452

Those closest to the fire spoke well, but the farther a group was away from the coals, | 456
the more jumbled their speech became. According to legend, that is why Native
American's speak different languages.

---

words per minute (wpm): _____   **minus errors:** _____ **= total wpm:** _____

THE THEFT OF FIRE - VERSION 1
COMPREHENSION ASSESSMENT

Directions: Circle the best answer.

1. According to the passage, where did the Miwok live?
    a. the San Joaquin Valley
    b. the Sierra Nevada Mountains
    c. neither the San Joaquin Valley nor the Sierra Nevada Mountains
    d. both the San Joaquin Valley and the Sierra Nevada Mountains

2. Who saw fire first?
    a. Coyote
    b. Lizard
    c. Rattlesnake
    d. Bear

3. Who stole fire from the Valley Assembly?
    a. Eagle
    b. Rain
    c. Flute-player
    d. Coyote

4. Who guarded the front door of the Valley Assembly?
    a. Eagle, Mountain Lion and Bear
    b. Eagle, Mountain Lion and Coyote
    c. Bear, Mountain Lion and Rattlesnake
    d. Lizard, Coyote and Mountain Lion

5. Who did the Valley Assembly summon to get their fire back?
    a. Wind, Clouds and Rain
    b. Storm, Rain and Clouds
    c. Hail, Clouds and Wind
    d. Wind, Rain and Hail

6. According to the passage, those closest to the fire spoke:
    a. jumbled
    b. Miwok
    c. Differently
    d. well

THE THEFT OF FIRE 1
A Miwok Myth Adapted from Stories by Thomas Williams (1917)
ACTIVE LISTENING AUDIENCE SHEET

Instructions: As you watch the skit, listen for words below. Put a hashmark at the end of the definition - each time that word is said.

WORDS

Joaquin: (wa-**keen**): A river, county and area in California. San Joaquin River, San Joaquin County, San Joaquin Valley.

Montezuma: (mon-t*uh*-**zoo**-m*uh*): A former town in Solano County, California. Also, Aztec emperors.

Tuolumne: (toe-**wall**-um-me): A town and county in California.

assembly: (*uh*-**sem**-blee): A coming together of people.

distribute: (dih-strib-yoot): To divide and give out in shares.

After the readers theater: Using the words above, write a short summary of what you saw.

_____

_____

_____

_____

_____

_____

_____

_____

_____

_____

_____

_____

_____

_____

Readers Theater
Fluency and Comprehension

THE THEFT OF FIRE - VERSION 2

Adapted from a Miwok Myth as told by William Fuller (1917)

CCSSRI: Read closely to determine what the text says explicitly and to make logical inferences from it; cite specific textual evidence when writing or speaking to support conclusions drawn from the text.

The Miwok consist of people from four distinct regions in central California: lake, coast, bay and interior. "Miwok" is the Central Sierra word meaning "people." Spanning from the coast directly north of San Francisco, inland southeast of Clear Lake to the central valley and into the Sierra Nevada – the Miwok are four linguistically related Native American groups. Their native languages are part of the Utian family and are considered endangered.

The Miwok did not have a centralized political system, but rather lived in small bands. They were primarily hunters and gatherers; however, they did harvest tobacco and keep dogs as pets.

The Sierra Miwok harvested acorns from the California Black Oak. Several of the black oak forests in Yosemite are the result of the trees cultivated by the Miwok. The Miwok also ate a variety of vegetables, bulbs, seeds, fruits and fungi. Animals were hunted and grasshoppers were a highly prized cuisine.

According to the California Parks Department, deer were the most important animal resource and all parts were used – to eat and to wear. Additionally, antlers and bones were used for tools and instruments.

The Miwok were and are a diverse group of people – rich in culture and diverse in traditions.

Third Read Questions

The main idea of the article is: _____
_____

Summarize the article. Be sure to use details.

_____
_____
_____
_____
_____
_____
_____
_____

THE THEFT OF FIRE – VERSION 2

Adapted from a Miwok Myth as told by William Fuller (1917) – 4.0 Reading Level

Lizard laid on a rock and saw smoke in the valley below him. "My grandmother	15
always starts a single fire to cook acorns. It's very lonely," he said to himself.	30
Coyote was passing and overheard Lizard talking to himself. "Then let's bring it	43
company," he said, then Coyote called for Mouse.	51
Mouse scurried over to the rocks, "What is it Coyote?"	61
"Lizard sees smoke in the valley. Go down and bring some here," Coyote answered.	75
"It'll be a long journey. How many flutes should I bring?" Mouse asked.	88
They all agreed two flutes would be enough, so off mouse went.	100
The journey was long. When Mouse got to the valley assembly, he was welcomed.	114
Mouse asked if he could play for the Valley Miwok and they welcomed his music. They	130
covered the door with a feather mat to keep the cold out.	142
Mouse played and played. He played until the valley people fell asleep. When Mouse	156
was sure they were all snoring, he filled his two flutes with fire. He cut his way out of the	176
Roundhouse by chopping through the feather mat.	183
When the valley people awoke, they noticed a portion of their fire was gone. They	198
called Hail and Rain.	202
"Mouse, from the mountains high, has taken some of our fire. You are the swiftest in	218
all the nations. Go and bring it back," the valley people commanded.	230
"We will hurry," Hail and Rain replied in unison.	239
Mouse was nearly up the hill when Rain and Hail caught up with him. Mouse hid his	256
flutes in a buckeye tree.	261
"You stole some of the Valley people's fire," Hail and Rain accused angrily.	274
Mouse held out his hands. "I have no fire. See?"	284
Hail and Rain looked at Mouse for a long time - finally they left.	297
Mouse took one of the flutes, but left the other in the buckeye tree.	311
Mouse ran into his roundhouse called out, "I have fire, but I only have one flute. Rain	328
and Hail followed me. They took the other one."	337
"One is enough," Great Bear said.	343
Mouse made a large fire in the center. It was then the people farthest from the center	360
lost their language. Those closest to the fire spoke correctly.	370
Those to the north spoke in a different way. Those from the south, east and west	386
spoke differently from each other.	391
Coyote walked to the center and put out the fire. As punishment, Coyote was	405
banished. He had to live outside and eat his meat cold. According to legend, that is also	422
why the Native American people speak different languages.	430

words per minute (wpm): _____   **minus errors:** _____ **= total wpm:** _____

THE THEFT OF FIRE – VERSION 2
Comprehension Assessment

Directions: Circle the best answer.

1. According to the passage, who cooked acorns alone?
    a. Lizard's mother
    b. Lizard's grandmother
    c. Lizard
    d. Coyote

2. In Version 2 of "The Theft of Fire," how many flutes did Mouse bring with him on his journey to the valley?
    a. one
    b. two
    c. three
    d. four

3. At the Valley Assembly, Mouse played until what happened?
    a. the Valley Assembly gave him fire
    b. the Valley Assembly kicked him out
    c. the Valley Assembly fell asleep
    d. Hail and Rain chased him

4. When Hail and Rain caught up with Mouse, where did he hide his flutes?
    a. in the river
    b. in the assembly hall
    c. behind his back
    d. in a buckeye tree

5. When Mouse told his people he only had one flute left, who told him one was enough?
    a. Bear
    b. Coyote
    c. Lizard
    d. Rain

6. How was Coyote punished for being greedy?
    a. He had to sleep outside
    b. He had to eat his food uncooked
    c. Both a and b
    d. Neither a nor b

THE THEFT OF FIRE – VERSION 2

Adapted from a Miwok Myth as told by William Fuller (1917)

ACTIVE LISTENING AUDIENCE SHEET

Instructions: Write down one descriptive word each character says:

NARRATOR 1:	**NARRATOR 2:**
LIZARD:	**COYOTE:**
MOOSE:	**VALLEY PERSON 1:**
VALLEY PERSON 2:	**HAIL:**
RAIN:	**GREAT BEAR:**

Instructions: Use the descriptive words you wrote above to write your own legend. Attach additional paper if you need to.

_____

_____

_____

_____

_____

_____

_____

_____

_____

_____

_____

_____

_____

_____

_____

_____

_____

_____

Readers Theater
Fluency and Comprehension

Legend of Choo'-too-se-ka' and Tis-sa'-sak

Adapted from a Myth of the Miwoks of Yosemite Valley

Legend of To-tau-kon-nu'-la and Tis-sa'-sak
From the Miwoks of the Yosemite Valley

The Native American legend from which the readers theater "Legend of To'tau-kon-'nu'la and Tis-sa'-sak, is based upon – is one version of how Half Dome, also known as Tis-sa'-sac", got its name.

The myth also proports that the figure of a man in a flowing robe – with one hand extended west -- can be seen on the mountain's face. The Miwok believe this to be the great Chieftain of the Ah-wah-nee Valley.

Similarly on the flat side of Half Dome, the face of Tis-sa'-sak can be seen. She is recognized by the way her dark hair is cut straight across her forehead and falls down at the sides.

In the photograph, at left, the light happened to be shining through the clouds, right on Tis-sa'-sak, the day this photograph was taken – in May 2018. Can you see her?

Legends and myths give us insight into the values, customs and experiences of past generations. In them, are clues to how people lived and what mattered to them. They are the earliest stories of our ancestors.

That said, there are universal themes in myths and legends that unite us all.

Think and Write: Why do you think myths and legends important today?

_____
_____
_____
_____
_____
_____
_____
_____

http://www.sacred-texts.com/nam/ca/ioy/ioy10.htm#fr_2 (September 16, 2018

Legend of Choo'-too-se-ka' and Tis-sa'-sak
Adapted from a Myth of the Miwoks of Yosemite Valley – 2.8 Reading Level

The Great Spirit led a band of his chosen people into the mountains. He told	15
them to rest in the beautiful Valley of Ah-wah-nee. In the Valley, they found an	30
abundance of food. The streams held swarms of fish. The meadows were high in	44
sweet clover and herds of deer and other game roamed the forests. The valley	58
floor held an endless supply of acorns, nuts, wild fruit and berries.	70
One day, their chief had a son. The elders wanted the boy to grow up to be	87
the greatest chief in all the lands. The boy was fed the meat of fish, so that he	105
grew to be a strong swimmer. He was fed the flesh of the deer, so that he might	123
be swift and light on his feet. He was fed the eggs of the mighty crane, so he	141
grew to be keen of sight. He was wrapped in the skin of a grizzly, so he grew to	160
be fearless and strong in combat.	166
The young chief was a kind and giving leader; because of this his people	180
called him him Choo'-too-se-ka' – meaning Supreme Good. He grew rich from	191
the gifts brought to him from all the lands and he shared those gifts with his	207
people. He also respected and revered the Great Spirit. In turn, the Great Spirit	221
showered his people with blessings.	226
He was so loved that his people built a great house for him at the base of To-	243
tau-kon-nu'-la – which today, is called El Capitan in Yosemite National Park.	254
One day, a group of people he'd never seen before entered the valley. With	268
them was the most beautiful woman the chief had ever seen.	279
"We would love to see your beautiful valley," the young maiden said as she	293
presented Choo'-too'-se-ka' with gifts of colorful beads and bright baskets.	303
Choo'-too'-se-ka' welcomed them. For the maiden, he built a grand house at	315
the base of what is now Half Dome in Yosemite. The young maiden, called Tis-	329
sa'-sak, showed his people how to weave baskets like the ones she brought to	344
them. She stayed for a long while and Choo'-too-se-ka' visited her everyday.	355
On one of his visits, he asked her to marry him. But she told him it was time	373
for her to return to her people. He bid her to think about it. When he returned	390
the next day, she was gone.	396
Choo'-too-se-ka' was so lonely – he left in search of her. In his village, the	410
crops failed, a drought came and then a great flood. His people where doomed.	424
The Great Spirit grew angry with Tis-sa'-sak and quaked the earth – splitting	436
half dome in two, then he brought abundance back to his chosen people.	449

words per minute (wpm): _____ **minus errors:** _____ **= total wpm:** _____

Legend of Choo'-too-se-ka' and Tis-sa'-sak
Comprehension Assessment

Directions: Circle the best answer.

1. According to the passage, who brought his chosen people into the Valley?
    a. Choo-too-se-ka'
    b. The Great Spirit
    c. Tis-sa'-sak
    d. Ah-wah-nee

2. What was the young chief fed to grow keen of sight?
    a. the eggs of a crane
    b. meat of fish
    c. flesh of deer
    d. acorn, nuts and berries

3. The passage states Choo-too-se-ka' means:
    a. Supreme Spirit
    b. Supreme Valley
    c. Supreme Good
    d. Supreme Ah-wah-nee

4. What gifts did the visitors bring?
    a. colorful beads and bright baskets
    b. acorns, nuts and berries
    c. colorful beads and berries
    d. bright baskets, colorful beads and acorn recipes

5. Choo-too-se-ka' built the young maiden a house at the base of:
    a. the valley of Ah-wah-nee
    b. what is now Half Dome
    c. El Capitan
    d. the base of Yosemite

6. The Great Spirit became angry so he:
    a. brought a flood
    b. brought a drought
    c. made the maiden leave the valley
    d. made the earth quake

Legend of Choo'-too-se-ka' and Tis-sa'-sak
Adapted from a Myth of the Miwoks of Yosemite Valley
Active Listening Audience Sheet

Instructions: Write your classmates' names next to the part he/she is playing, then write down two character traits for each character.

Narrator 1:	Narrator 2:
Narrator 2:	Little Deer:
Gray Fox:	Shining Star:
Sitting Moon:	Great Spirit:
Chief:	Little Lamb:
Young Chieftain (Choo'-too-se-ka'):	Tis-sa'-ack:
Elder 1:	Elder 2:
Running Bear:	Young Chieftain/ Choo'-too-se-ka':

Readers Theater
Fluency and Comprehension

Why Native Americans Have So Many Tribes

Adapted from a Virginia Algonquian Legend about the Origin of the Tribes

The Powhatan

The Powhatan are also known as the Virginia Algonquians. It is estimated that there were between 14,000 and 21,000 Powhatan people when the English colonized Jamestown in 1607.

The Powhatan lived in Tidewater, Virginia. They built their homes by bending small trees and placing woven mats or bark over the tops of the structures.

Th Powhatan' grew crops, most notably maize, or corn, but they hunted and fished the rich land of their great forest as well.

Villages were arranged around family ties. Each village was led by a chief. The chief could be male or female. Each local chief paid tribute to the great chief (Mamanatowick).

The Powhatan were all agriculturally oriented. They used the land, until they could use it no more and then they moved on. Clearing another parcel by fire. Moving often.

The Powhatan way of life changed greatly after the English arrived.

Answer the following questions:

1. According to the passage, how many Powhatans lived in Virginia before the English arrived?
   a. 2,000 to 3,000
   b. 1,400 to 2,100
   c. 140 to 211
   d. 14,000 to 21,000

2. Powhatan homes are made from:
   a. thick pieces of tree bark leaned against one another
   b. bending small trees and covering them with mats or bark
   c. standing up poles and using animal skins as roofing
   d. making lean-to shelters in the thick forests

3. Use the information in the passage to describe the Powhatan way of life.

_____

_____

_____

_____

_____

Why Native Americans Have So Many Tribes
Adapted from a Virginia Algonquian Legend about the Origin of the Tribes – 4.0 Grade Level

Many moons ago, so many that one cannot count them all, all of the people lived	16
underground. They lived in total darkness with their animals. Animals and people lived	29
in harmony as one.	33
One of the animals was very brave. It was the ground mole. One day the mole	49
crawled far, far away from the others. It crawled up and up. After a long time, it saw a	68
hole. The mole crawled out of it and saw light. It saw a spectacular sky. It saw tall trees	87
which seemed to touch the white fluffy clouds. It saw glimmering lakes and sparkling	101
streams.	102
"There is no darkness here. Here there is only beauty and light," Mole said to himself.	118
Mole crawled back through the hole as fast as it could. Mole told all of the animals	135
and all of the people of the wonders he saw. Mole was stumbling around, for the light	152
had blinded him. This is why moles are blind to this day.	164
The people were so excited. There was light out there. There was beauty out there.	179
They could hardly wait to go out and see for themselves.	190
One by one, the animals and the people climbed out of the hole. The people saw the	207
world, and all of the beauty it encompassed, for the first time. More and more people	223
came out of the hole into the wonderful world.	232
Then something horrible happened. Someone got stuck while trying to pass through	244
the hole. The people pushed from the inside and pulled from the outside, but the person	260
would not budge. Some of the people did not leave the darkness.	272
Soon, the people outside came to a river and a bird flew over. The waters parted and	289
some passed. When the waters came back together, some did not get across. After many	304
moons, those who did cross came to the base of majestic mountains – so tall they seemed	319
to reach the sky. A kind deer led them over the mountains, but an eagle chased the deer	337
away and some did not cross, so they made their home at the base of the mountains.	354
Those who crossed, found themselves in a forest so thick – they could not see each	369
other. They tried to stay together, but they could not.	379
A few went this way and a few went that way. All over the place they scattered. And	397
to this day, they all live in different places.	406

words per minute (wpm): _____   **minus errors:** _____   **= total wpm:** _____

Why Native Americans Have So Many Tribes
Comprehension Assessment

Directions: Circle the best answer.

1. According to the passage, how many moons ago did the people live underground?
    a. many moons
    b. ten moons
    c. moons and moons back to the beginning of time
    d. so many you couldn't count them all

2. According to the legend, which animal went out into the light first?
    a. Lizard
    b. Eagle
    c. Mole
    d. Deer

3. Why was the animal who first went above ground stumbling around?
    a. he lost sight of the deer
    b. the eagle blinded him
    c. underground was dark
    d. the light blinded him

4. What parted the water?
    a. a flying bird
    b. a swimming trout
    c. a running deer
    d. a soaring eagle

5. According to the Legend, why did some stay underground?
    a. the light blinded them
    b. they lost sight of the deer
    c. the waters closed up again
    d. someone got stuck in the hole

6. What chased the deer away?
    a. a bird
    b. an eagle
    c. a mole
    d. a deer

Why Native Americans Have So Many Tribes
Adapted from a Virginia Algonquian Legend About the Origin of the Tribes
Active Listening Audience Sheet

Instructions: Write your classmates name next to the part he/she is playing.

Write one word that describes both the character your classmate is playing and your classmate.

Mole 1:	Mole 2:
Algonquian 1:	Algonquian 2:
Algonquian 3:	Algonquian 4:
Algonquian 5:	Algonquian 6
Algonquian 7:	Algonquian 8:
Young Algonquian:	Narrator 1:
Narrator 2:	Narrator 3:

Readers Theater
Fluency and Comprehension

How the Deer Got His Horns

Adapted from a Cherokee Legend

Cherokee Children

In the earliest days, the Cherokee Nation was divided into clans, rather than tribes. These clans shared everything - even raising children. Each person in the clan played a vital role in the life of every child and each child was important to every citizen.

Children played an essential role in the traditional Cherokee culture and each clan took very good care of its children. This began with the mother. A Cherokee baby was primarily cared for by its mother. Babies were bathed in warm water daily and then rubbed with animal oil. They were coddled and rarely left their mother's side.

Older girls remained in the care of the women in their clan. These older women were looked to for advice and were highly valued.

When boys were very young, the oldest "uncle" took over their education. At about eight-years-old, boys were expected to know how to use a blowgun and help bring in food for the family. Cherokee boys played sports. Wrestling, weight-lifting, and ball playing competitions were frequent.

Both boys and girls were taught to respect their elders and listen to their wise words. Children were well-versed in the traditions, history and spiritual matters of their clan.

The Cherokee valued children and treated them with respect, thus Cherokee children learned by example to be respectful and care for others.

Answer the following questions:

1. According to the passage, the Cherokee Nation was not divided into tribes, but was divided into what kind of group instead?
    a. clans
    b. families
    c. states
    d. nations

2. Cherokee children were taught:
    a. to respect and listen to their elders
    b. to be great chiefs
    c. to play rather than work
    d. to never leave their family

3. Summarize the passage.

_____
_____
_____
_____
_____

How the Deer Got His Horns
Adapted from a Cherokee Legend – Reading Level 3.5

Long, long ago deer had no horns, but rather his head was as smooth as a doe's head.	18
Deer was a great runner and Rabbit was a great jumper. All of the animals were curious	35
to know which could go farther in the same amount of time.	47
They talked about it and talked about it, until finally they arranged a match between	62
the two. The prize was to be a great pair of antlers. The deer and the rabbit were to start	82
from the same place and go from one side of a thicket to another. Whoever came in first	100
would win the antlers.	104
On the day of the race all of the animals were there. The antlers were put down on the	123
ground to mark the starting point of the race.	132
While everyone was admiring the horns, Rabbit said: "I don't know this part of the	147
land. I want to walk through the bushes to see where I am going to run."	163
The other animals said that it was all right for Rabbit to take a look.	178
Rabbit went into the thicket. The other animals waited and waited and waited, but	192
rabbit did not come out. The other animals sent a messenger to look for him. The	208
messenger found Rabbit gnawing down the bushes. Rabbit had gnawed so far, he'd	221
cleared a path to the other side.	228
The messenger turned around quietly and went back and told the others.	240
When Rabbit came out, they accused him of cheating. He denied it – until the other	255
animals went into the thicket and saw the cleared path. They agreed that Rabbit was a	271
trickster and had no right to enter the race at all. They gave the antlers to Deer.	288
They told Rabbit that since he liked gnawing down the bushes so much – he had to	304
do it forever. And so he does – to this very day. And to this very day, male deer have	323
antlers.	324

words per minute (wpm): _____   **minus errors:** _____ **= total wpm:** _____

How the Deer Got His Horns

Comprehension Assessment

Directions: Circle the best answer.

1. According to the passage, long ago which animal had no horns?
    a. Rabbit
    b. Coyote
    c. Deer
    d. Lizard

2. To see who could go farther fastest, what did the animals decide to do?
    a. have a race
    b. have a hopping match
    c. gnaw through a thicket
    d. talk it out

3. What was to be the prize?
    a. a thicket
    b. to be named leader of all animals
    c. a trophy
    d. antlers

4. Who cheated?
    a. Deer
    b. Rabbit
    c. Eagle
    d. Mountain Lion

5. The main idea of the passage is:
    a. Cheaters never win.
    b. If you go into a thicket, don't clear a path.
    c. You don't need antlers to be a winner.
    d. The fastest is always the best.

6. Summarize the passage in one or two sentences:

    _____

    _____

    _____

How the Deer Got His Horns
Adapted from a Cherokee Legend
Active Listening Audience Sheet

Instructions: Circle each word when you hear it the first time, put a check mark under the word, each time it is said again.

daughter	somersaulting
farther	thicker
antlers	together
trickster	ashamed
flopping	creature

Readers Theater
Fluency and Comprehension

The Legend of the No-Face Doll

Adapted from the Haudenosaunee, or Six Nations, People

The Legend of the No-Face Doll

Adapted from a Legend of the Haudenosaunee, or Six Nations, People

Active Listening Audience Sheet

Instructions: Write down one descriptive word each character says:

Narrator 1:	Narrator 2:
Wind:	Beans Spirit:
Squash Spirit:	Corn Spirit:
Villager 1:	Girl Villager:
Great Spirit:	Haudenosaunee Girl:

Instructions: Use the descriptive words you wrote in a paragraph that tells what you liked or didn't like about "The Legend of the No-Face Doll."

_____
_____
_____
_____
_____
_____
_____
_____
_____
_____
_____
_____
_____
_____
_____
_____
_____
_____

Six Nations

The Native Americans of upper New York and southeastern Canada were called the Iroquois by early settlers and are considered to have the world's oldest surviving participatory democracy. Today, they call themselves the Haudenosaunee, or Six Nations, People and are still a model of peace and unity. In fact, their constitution is believed to have been one of the models used by the framers when writing the U.S. Constitution in 1787.

Benjamin Franklin was interested in the Haudenosaunee government structure and balance of power and studied it extensively. Franklin then brought his research to the Constitutional Convention.

Where did the Haudenosaunee constitution come from? According to their traditional Peacemaker story, the separate groups that comprise the nations, warred with each other for decades. They came together around 1600, to live in peace after their chief Hiawatha, who was mourning the loss of his love, joined with Dekanawidah to unify the tribes. Dekanawidah was a peacemaker who managed to join together the warring Haudenosaunee Nations – and helped develop their Great Law of Peace (Gayanesshagowa).

A group of 50 peace chiefs still gather today. They meet in the traditional longhouse, which is what the word Haudenosaunee means. The 50 peace chiefs are made up of members from the six nations: the Mohawk, the Oneida, the Onondaga, the Cayuga, the Seneca and the Tuscarora.

Answer the following questions:

1. The Six Nations are considered to have one of the:
   a. greatest peace stories of all time
   b. best longhouses in the world
   c. world's oldest participatory democracy
   d. best war plan in the world

2. Haudenosaunee means:
   a. peacemaker
   b. great chief
   c. constitution
   d. longhouse

3. What is the main idea of the passage "Six Nations?" Use complete sentences for your answer.

_____

_____

_____

_____

The Legend of the No-Face Doll
Adapted from the Haudenosaunee, or Six Nations, People – Reading Level 4.4

To this day, the Haudenosaunee people do not put faces on their corn husk dolls.	15
Here's why:	17
One day the Great Spirit of the Haudenosaunee people called together Corn, Beans	30
and Squash and told them they were to be the Sustainers of Life. The three were	46
honored; Corn Spirit was so excited to be one of the Sustainers of Life that she asked the	64
Great Spirit if there was anything more she could do for her people.	77
The Great Spirit told her she could make a doll from her own husk. Eagerly, the Corn	94
Spirit made the doll and gave it a beautiful face. The Beans Spirit and the Corn Spirit	111
told her that her doll truly had the most beautiful face they'd ever seen.	125
The Corn Spirit took the doll from village to village, so all of the children could play	142
with it. Everywhere she went, people told her how beautiful the doll was. It was not	158
long before she became conceited.	163
One day, on her journey, she passed a clear, still pool of water and caught her own	180
reflection. "I am as beautiful as my doll," she told herself. Soon she began to think she	197
was better than everyone else.	202
The Great Spirit grew angry. He summoned the Corn Spirit to him and told her if she	219
continued to think she was better than others, a terrible punishment would befall her .	233
Corn Spirit begged to know what would happen, but the Great Spirit refused to tell	248
her.	249
Corn Spirit continued her travels with her doll. Again, village after village told her	263
how wonderful the doll was and how beautiful her face was. And, before long, the Corn	279
Spirit grew conceited again.	283
The Great Spirit called the Corn Spirit before it. "I warned you once, but you did not	300
listen. A punishment the likes you've never seen will now come upon you."	313
"Oh please, Great Spirit, I am so sorry. What is the punishment?" Corn Spirit asked.	328
Still, he would not tell her.	334
Corn Spirit left the lodge and passed a clear pool of water. She stopped to admire	350
herself and gasped! She had no face. The Great Spirit had taken it away.	364
The Haudenosaunee still do not put faces on their corn husk dolls to remind people	379
to never think they are better than anyone else.	388

words per minute (wpm): _____   minus errors: _____ = total wpm: _____

The Legend of the No-Face Doll
Comprehension Assessment

Directions: Circle the best answer.

1. According to the Legend, which spirits are the "Sustainers of Life?"
    a. Corn, Bean and Squash
    b. Corn, Beans and Squash
    c. The Great Spirit
    d. Corn and Squash

2. Who asked the Great Spirit if there was more it could do?
    a. Corn
    b. Beans
    c. Bean
    d. Squash

3. Which spirit took the doll from village to village?
    a. Squash
    b. Bean
    c. Corn
    d. Beans

4. What displeased the Great Spirit?
    a. Corn Spirit grew conceited
    b. the doll had no face
    c. the "Sustainers of Life" went from village to village
    d. the Great Spirit was not angry

5. How many warnings did the Great Spirit give?
    a. none
    b. one
    c. two
    d. three

6. What was the punishment the Great Spirit gave?
    a. the Great Spirit said dolls could not have faces
    b. he took Corn Spirit's face
    c. he took Squash Spirit's face
    d. he told the three they could no longer be "Sustainers of Life"

How to Make a Corn Husk Doll

The following sets of instructions are simple to follow and tested on real fourth graders. The step-by-step photographs are renderings of a fourth grader making the dolls. Corn husk dolls are simple to make and are a great activity to add to or replace the traditional Thanksgiving classroom party – as corn husk dolls were made by both Native Americans and early settlers

Hint: Purchasing corn husks can be expensive. A great team building activity for the first day of school is to plant corn in paper cups. When corn is large enough – transplant to an area outside, select students to water and weed and harvest your own stalks. Or - if available – corn farms, fruit stands and even grocery stores may donate husks or corn stalks for your whole class.

Materials:

6 to 10 corn husks per student
twine, yarn or raffia
scissors
fabric – the most economical way to obtain fabric for classroom use is to put out a letter to parents asking for large fabric remnants and clean, old sheets they do not want back. While it would be great to have the colorful felt called for in most instructions – it is not always in a teacher's budget and any fabric (old t-shirts, dish towels, etc.) works just fine.

Corn Husk Doll - Method 1

1. Assemble materials.

2. Line up corn husks and bend in the center. Tie off 1-2 inches from bend for head.

3. Separate some 2-3 corn husks and tie off arm one.

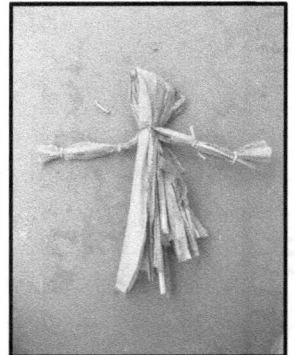

4. Separate corn husks and tie off arm two.

5. Separate legs into equal parts and tie towards top of both legs.

6. Tie off legs towards the bottom to make feet for a boy doll.

7. Cut fabric and design an outfit.

How to Make a Corn Husk Doll
Method Two

1. Assemble materials.

2. Separate and roll two husks. Tie off ends. These are your arms.

3. Tie off the top of the rest of the husks approximately 2 inches from the top.

4. Bring one piece of husk over the top and tie off.

5. Separate the body in two equal parts and put in the arms.

6. Tie off the center of the body for a girl doll.

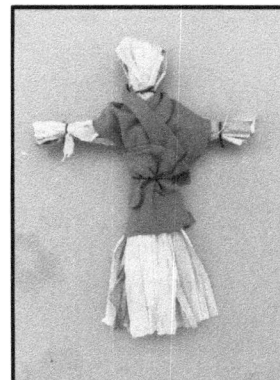

7. Dress as desired

Readers Theater
Fluency and Comprehension

THE CORN SPIRIT READERS THEATER

Based on a Tuscarora Harvest Legend

THE CORN SPIRIT READERS THEATER
Based on a Tuscarora Harvest Legend
ACTIVE LISTENING AUDIENCE SHEET

Instructions: As you watch the skit, listen for the following words –
underline each word when it is spoken.

ancestor	autumn	substantial
single	corn	horrible
fields	stumble	thought
torn	lodge	community
daughters	abundance	disappeared

Choose the two words you think best describe the "The Corn Spirit
Readers Theater" and use them in a sentence telling why you think they
best represent the skit.

_____

_____

_____

_____

THE CORN SPIRIT READERS THEATER
Based on a Tuscarora Harvest Legend – Reading Level 3.5

Long, long ago, there was a village of people whose cornfields were blessed with	15
bountiful harvests. Year after year, they had so much corn that they began to take it for	32
granted and neglect their fields. They stopped weeding and let the children trample the	46
cornstalks as they played.	50
When harvest came, the villagers left corn on the stocks. They wasted more than they	65
used. They even threw corn to their dogs. They dried some for winter, but not like they	82
had in the past.	86
The storage baskets, to hold the corn for the winter, were poorly made and not buried	102
deeply enough. The people had grown lazy and did everything carelessly.	113
There was such an abundance of food that they didn't even care if there was enough	129
corn for the winter. They stopped showing respect for the corn that gave them	143
sustenance and forgot to thank the Creator for all that was provided to them.	157
Everyone, that is, but one man: Dayohagwenda. Dayohagwenda cared for his fields,	169
picked all of his corn, made his baskets well and stored away his winter supply with	185
care. He looked at the others with great sadness in his heart.	197
That autumn, when the people went hunting, all of the game had vanished from the	221
forest. They tired to fish, but the streams and lakes were empty. When they dug up their	229
corn stores, they found that their poorly made baskets had rotted away. The ones that	244
didn't rot were filled with mice.	250
"What are we going to do?" cried the people. "We will surely starve."	263
At the same time, Dayohagwenda was walking in the forest. He came across an old	278
trail he had never been on before. The trail led to a clearing, in its center, was an old	297
lodge with weeds growing all around it and an old man – kneeling beside it – crying.	312
Dayohagwenda asked the old man why he was crying and why were his clothes	326
tattered and dirty and why were there so many weeds around his lodge.	339
The old man told Dayohagwenda that he cried because his people had forgotten him.	353
His clothes were torn because his people threw him to the dogs. There were weeds all	369
around, because his people did not take care of him.	379
Then it hit Dayohagwenda. The old man was the Corn Spirit.	390
The Corn Spirit told Dayohagwenda that he was going to go away and never return,	405
because his people had forsaken him.	411
Dayohagwenda begged for another chance for his people. It was granted, but the Corn	425
Spirit told Dayohagwenda: "If our people show me respect, I will not leave."	438
Dayohagwenda went back to his people and told them the story. They told him they	453
were going to starve and explained how their corn had rotted and how there was	468
nothing left to eat.	472
"I spoke with the Corn Spirit and if you show him respect, he will stay and grant us	490
all his blessings," Dayohagwenda told them. "Come and I will share my corn."	503
When they dug up Dayohagwenda's corn – there was more there than he had buried.	517
There was enough to carry the whole village through the winter.	428
To this day, the people give thanks for all of the blessings they have and never forget	445
the Corn Spirit.	448

words per minute (wpm): _____   **minus errors:** _____ **= total wpm:** _____

THE CORN SPIRIT READERS THEATER
Comprehension Assessment

Directions: Circle the best answer.

1. According to the beginning of the Legend, the people did all of the following except:
   a. trample their corn
   b. show thanks for their corn
   c. throw their corn to their dogs
   d. make their baskets weak

2. Who did the people of the village stop showing respect for?
   a. Dayohagwenda
   b. their dogs
   c. the Creator
   d. the Corn Spirit

3. Dayohagwenda was walking in the forest and came upon:
   a. an old lodge
   b. an abundance of corn
   c. an old man who was sighing
   d. an abundance of game

4. According to the legend, who was the old man?
   a. Dayohagwenda
   b. the Creator
   c. the Corn Spirit
   d. their leader

5. Summarize the legend using complete sentences.

_____

_____

_____

_____

_____

_____

_____

Tuscarora Culture and History Warm-Up

When we think about Native Americans, we often think of them only in the past; however, Native Americans, like the Tuscarora have a vibrant present and future as well.

The Tuscarora people are part of the Six Nations. The name "Tuscarora" comes from the word "hemp people" in their native language. Hemp is a milkweed that produces fibers similar to those of the cotton plant. The Tuscarora used hemp to make cloth for shirts, rope and ceremonial objects.

The Tuscarora are originally from North Carolina; however, after the Tuscarora War in the early 1700s, many were enslaved by British settlers or killed. Those who remained moved north to live in New York with their relatives of the powerful Haudenosaunee. The Tuscarora were the last people to join the Kanonsionni - or league of clans - that form the Six Nations; however, they were the first native people to be dispossessed of their land during colonialization.

Today, most Tuscarora live in New York and Ontario, Canada and continue as a sovereign nation with the Haudenosaunee government - which includes chiefs, clan mothers and faith keepers. They work to maintain their traditions; however, their language is considered endangered; because, their children no longer learn to speak it. They continue to play lacrosse, or stickball", as a way to settle disputes without war.

Answer the following questions:

1. What does the word Tuscarora mean?
   a. hemp
   b. Haudenosaunee
   c. clan
   d. North Carolina

2. Where are the Tuscarora originally from?
   a. New York
   b. North Carolina
   c. Britain
   d. Ontario

3. The Tuscarora were the first native people to be:
   a. colonized
   b. dispossessed
   c. settled
   d. Maintained

4. What do the Tuscarora play to settle disputes?
   a. football
   b. soccer
   c. lacrosse
   d. polo

Hasbrouck & Tindal Oral Reading Fluency Chart

Grade	Percentile	Fall WCPM	Winter WCPM	Spring WCPM
3	90	128	146	162
	75	99	120	137
	50	71	92	107
	25	44	62	78
	10	21	36	48
4	90	145	166	180
	75	119	139	152
	50	94	112	123
	25	68	87	98
	10	45	61	72
5	90	166	182	194
	75	139	156	168
	50	110	127	139
	25	85	99	109
	10	61	74	83
6	90	177	195	204
	75	153	167	177
	50	127	140	150
	25	98	111	122
	10	68	82	93

The chart at right contains the National Fluency Norms based on research from Hasbrouck and Tindal (2004). Their extensive study of Oral Fluency, "Oral Reading Fluency: 90 Years of Measurement," is available on the University of Oregon's website.

It was also published in "The Reading Teacher" (2006).

The chart shows mean reading oral fluency rates for grade levels 3-6, by percentile, for fall, winter and spring. The chart is widely used to rate oral reading fluency.

Students scoring below the 50th percentile using the average score of two unpracticed readings from grade-level materials need a fluency-building program.

Instructions for Reading Fluency Passages:
1. Copy and distribute the same passage to each student.
2. Read the passage together once (this step may be skipped).
3. Partner students and explain the instructions:
   1. Students are going to take turns reading each passage.
   2. You are going to set a timer for one minute.
   3. One student will read, while the other follows along – marking words pronounced incorrectly. When the timer sounds, the reader will keep reading, but the person marking the paper will put an X through the last word read.
   4. Students will determine words read per minutes by:
      a) Use the numbers on the right side, then subtract mistakes made. Write solution to the equation on the total wpm line.

This exercise may also be used for fluency practice by pairing students with aids, as homework, or back table work by pairing strong readers with strugglers.

*wcpm=words correct per minute

Readers Theater
Fluency and Comprehension

READERS THEATERS SCRIPTS

NATIVE AMERICAN LEGEND ADAPTATIONS

THE THEFT OF FIRE - VERSION 1
A Miwok Myth Adapted from Stories by Thomas Williams (1917)

RUNNING TIME: SEVEN MINUTES
CHARACTERS – 15:

NARRATOR 1	NARRATOR 2	BLACK GOOSE 1	BLACK GOOSE 2
WHITE GOOSE 1	WHITE GOOSE 2	LIZARD	COYOTE
BEAR	FLUTE-PLAYER	RATTLESNAKE	LITTLE BEAR
EAGLE	HAIL	MOUNTAIN LION	

NARRATOR 1: The Miwok people lived in the great San Joaquin Valley and in the foothills of the Sierra Nevada Mountains.

NARRATOR 2: Long ago only the people who gathered in the assembly house of the San Joaquin River had fire….

NARRATOR 1: …while the people at the assembly house of the Geese, had none. The assembly house of the Geese was at Goodwin's Ranch, near Montezuma, Tuolumne County.

NARRATOR 2: The birds and the animals were all men and no one from the great foothills had fire.

BLACK GOOSE 1: White Goose, the Black Geese need your help.

WHITE GOOSE 1: I'll call everyone to the assembly hall. Meet us there.

NARRATOR 1: Meanwhile, Lizard lay on top of a large rock and looked down at the valley.

LIZARD: There's fire down there.

NARRATOR 2: Coyote happened to be walking by.

COYOTE: What's that you say?

LIZARD: Fire. They've fire in the valley and we have none.

COYOTE: The lies you tell Lizard. They've no fire.

LIZARD: Come and see for yourself.

NARRATOR 1: Coyote climbed up on the rock and Lizard pointed out to the great valley below.

COYOTE: I see no fire.

LIZARD: There! Look at the assembly house. See the sparks?

COYOTE: I can't even see the assembly hall.

LIZARD: There! Watch! There and another.

NARRATOR 2: Coyote went to the Geese.

COYOTE: Lizard sees fire coming from the great assembly hall in the valley.

BLACK GOOSE 1: I see no fire.

WHITE GOOSE 1: Neither do I.

COYOTE: I can't either, but Lizard says he can.

BLACK GOOSE 1: Lizard tells tall tales.

COYOTE: It's different this time. I can tell. I'm going back up to the rock. Maybe, the fire will be easier to see at sundown.

NARRATOR 1: Coyote went back to the rock and waited and waited and waited.

NARRATOR 2: Finally, when the sun was beyond the horizon - he saw it.

COYOTE: Why Lizard, you're right! They do have fire!

NARRATOR 1: Coyote went back to the assembly house.

COYOTE: I saw it! I saw the fire!

WHITE GOOSE 1: Then it's true?

BLACK GOOSE 1: We need some of their fire. Flute-player go down and look at the fire.

WHITE GOOSE 2: Then come back and tell us what you see.

BLACK GOOSE 2: And, hurry.

NARRATOR 2: Flute-player said nothing but took four flutes and journeyed into the valley.

NARRATOR 1: When he arrived - Bear, Rattlesnake and Mountain Lion guarded the door. Flute-player played for them.

BEAR: You can't enter here.

FLUTE-PLAYER: I just want to see the fire.

NARRATOR 2: They couldn't understand him.

RATTLESNAKE: Hisssss sssspppeech is not like ourssssss.

MOUNTAIN LION: I think he wants to see the fire.

FLUTE-PLAYER: May I come in?

MOUNTAIN LION: Be on your way little mouse.

NARRATOR 2: Flute-player went up to the top of the assembly house.

NARRATOR 1: Eagle had his wing over the smoke hole – blocking Flute-player's way.

FLUTE-PLAYER: Eagle? (Louder) Eagle? He's asleep on the job. But how do I get past his wing?

NARRATOR 2: Flute-player thought and though.

NARRATOR 1: Finally, he cut off two of the grand Eagle's feathers and quietly entered the assembly house.

FLUTE-PLAYER: They're all sleeping. I'll go to the fire and fill my flutes.

NARRATOR 2: As he left the assembly house, the people began to stir.

LITTLE BEAR: It is Flute-player from the hills and he's taken fire.

MOUNTAIN LION: Eagle! Flute-player took fire!

NARRATOR 1: The great Eagle looked to the sky and called:

EAGLE: Wind, Rain, Hail – go after Flute-player! Quickly! He has taken some of our fire.

NARRATOR 2: Hail caught up to Flute-player first.

FLUTE-PLAYER: Hail is on my tail. The river! I'll hide my flutes in the river.

HAIL: You have our fire.

FLUTE-PLAYER: I have nothing.

NARRATOR 1: Hail eyed Flute-player cautiously and then left.

FLUTE-PLAYER: My flutes. Fire are you still there?

NARRATOR 2: Flute player tooted, and sparks came out.

FLUTE-PLAYER: I have my fire, but Wind and Rain are making it weak.

NARRATOR 1: Flute-player traveled faster. Then he saw Coyote.

COYOTE: I was afraid something had happened to you.

FLUTE-PLAYER: I have fire. Run ahead and tell the others.

COYOTE: I'll gather them at the assembly hall.

NARRATOR 2: Coyote ran back to tell the others that Flute-player had fire.

NARRATOR 1: When Flute-player arrived home, Wind and Rain rolled back into the valley below.

NARRATOR 2: Flute-player climbed to the top of the assembly hall.

BLACK GOOSE 2: He's playing.

BLACK GOOSE 1: And coals are dropping.

WHITE GOOSE 1: We have fire in the center.

BLACK GOOSE 2: And we have it here, but not as much.

COYOTE: Keep playing. Over here. I have no fire.

NARRATOR 1: Flute-player dropped his last piece of coal in front of coyote.

NARRATOR 2: This meant some went without.

NARRATOR 1: Coyote was greedy and would not wait until the fire could be evenly distributed.

NARRATOR 2: The fire was more than something to cook on.

NARRATOR 1: The fire was more than something to keep them warm.

NARRATOR 2: It connected the people.

NARRATOR 1: Those closest to the fire spoke well.

NARRATOR 2: But the farther one was from the fire – the more jumbled the language got.

NARRATOR 1: That's why Native Americans speak different languages.

BLACK GOOSE 3: (to the audience) By stealing the fire – Flute-player saved my people from dying that winter.

WHITE GOOSE 3: Yes, but Coyote became impatient and took the last of the fire for himself, if he had not, we would all have spoken the same language.

BLACK GOOSE 3: And there would have been peace among all people.

WHITE GOOSE 3: Instead, by being greedy, Coyote brought fighting among people who did not speak the same language.

BLACK GOOSE 3: This is a legend of my people.

THE END

THE THEFT OF FIRE – VERSION 2
Adapted from a Miwok Myth as told by William Fuller (1917)

RUNNING TIME: FIVE MINUTES
CHARACTERS 10:

NARRATOR 1	NARRATOR 2	LIZARD	COYOTE
MOUSE	VALLEY PERSON 1	VALLEY PERSON 2	HAIL
RAIN	GREAT BEAR		

NARRATOR 1: Lizard laid on a rock and saw smoke in the valley below him.

LIZARD: My grandmother always starts a single fire to cook acorns. It's very lonely.

COYOTE: Then we'll bring it company. Mouse!

NARRATOR 1: Coyote called for Mouse, who was the assembly's flute-player.

MOUSE: What is it Coyote?

COYOTE: Go down into the valley and get fire.

MOUSE: It'll be a long journey, but I'll go. How many flutes should I take with me?

LIZARD: Two. Take two flutes.

COYOTE: Yes. Lizard is correct. Two flutes will be plenty.

NARRATOR 2: Mouse traveled from the mountains near Tuolumne to the Valley below. He arrived at the Valley Assembly and saw sparks coming from the Roundhouse.

VALLEY PERSON 1: Come in, Mouse.

VALLEY PERSON 2: Yes, come in. You are welcome here.

MOUSE: May I play for you?

VALLEY PERSON 1: Please play for us Mouse. Would you?

NARRATOR 1: Valley Person 1 covered the door with a feather mat.

VALLEY PERSON 2: That'll keep the cold out while you play.

VALLEY PERSON 1: You may begin at any time.

NARRATOR 2: Mouse played and played and did not stop playing until all of the Valley Assembly were asleep.

NARRATOR 1: They snored and snored. Mouse continued to play until he was sure every single person was sleeping.

NARRATOR 2: Then he went to the fire and took two coals, placing one in each flute.

NARRATOR 1: He cut his way through the feather mat that blocked the door and scurried up the mountains towards home.

NARRATOR 2: When the valley people awoke, they found Mouse gone and much of the fire gone with him.

VALLEY PERSON 3: Hail and Rain! Hurry! We need you.

NARRATOR 1: Hail and Rain appeared in a black cloud above.

HAIL: At your service, oh great one.

RAIN: We're here for whatever you need.

VALLEY PERSON 3: Mouse, from the mountains high, took some of our fire.

VALLEY PERSON 2: You are the swiftest of the valley people. Please. Hurry.

HAIL: Not to worry.

RAIN: We will find him, and fire will be restored in its entirety.

NARRATOR 2: Mouse was nearly up the mountain when he heard Hail and Rain come quickly behind him.

NARRATOR 1: Mouse threw his flutes into a buckeye tree just as Rain and Hail caught up with him.

RAIN: You stole our fire.

MOUSE: I did not.

HAIL: You stole our fire and must give it back.

NARRATOR 1: Mouse looked around and held out his hands.

MOUSE: I do not have your fire. See. I have nothing.

NARRATOR 2: Rain and Hail started the journey back down the hills to the valley.

MOUSE: That was a close one. I'll take my fire and go home.

NARRATOR 1: Mouse took one of the flutes back to his Assembly house and left one in the buckeye tree. Great Bear and all of the Assembly were waiting for him.

GREAT BEAR: Build a fire.

MOUSE: I only have one flute left. Rain chased me and caught me. It was a terrible fight. He took one flute.

GREAT BEAR: One is enough to build a fire.

NARRATOR 2: Mouse made a large fire. It was then the people lost their language. Those closest to the fire spoke correctly.

NARRATOR 1: Those to the north side of the Assembly House spoke in a broken way, but it was still the same language.

NARRATOR 2: Those at the south, east and west spoke differently than those in the north and differently from each other. This was because of the cold. The farther a group was from the fire, the more difficult they were to understand.

NARRATOR 1: Coyote came in and put out the fire.

GREAT BEAR: Coyote, why did you extinguish the fire?

NARRATOR 2: Coyote could not understand him.

GREAT BEAR: From this day forth, Coyote, you will eat your food outside and without fire.

NARRATOR 1: That is why Coyote always eats his meat uncooked.

NARRATOR 2: And that is why all of the Native American people speak different languages.

THE END

Legend of Choo'-too-se-ka' and Tis-sa'-sak
Adapted from a Myth of the Miwoks of the Yosemite Valley

Running Time: Six Minutes
Characters 16:

Narrator 1	Narrator 2	Narrator 3	Little Deer
Gray Fox	Shining Sky	Sitting Moon	Great Spirit
Chief	Little Lamb	Tis-sa'-ack	Elder 1
Elder 2	Running Bear	Young Chieftain/ Choo'-too-se-ka'	

Each person must announce their name and the character they are playing before the readers theater begins.

Narrator 1: Many moons and snows have passed since the Great Spirit led a small band of his favorite children into the Ah-wah'-nee Valley.

Narrator 2: Today, Ah-wah'-nee is the valley floor of Yosemite National Park, but long ago this band of chosen people stopped to rest from their wanderings.

Narrator 3: They were tired from years of traveling from a distant land separated by the great waters.

Little Deer: There is so much food here.

Gray Fox: And the rivers flow cold and are filled with fresh water and scrumptious trout. I will become a great fisherman.

Shining Sky: And I will gather sweet meadow clover and sour oxalis for medicine. Look around us. The trees and bushes are full of acorns and pine nuts.

Sitting Moon: And fruits and berries I've never seen before.

Little Deer: The forests have herds of deer and other animals for food and skins.

Narrator 1: They were grateful to the Great Spirit for bringing them to the valley that they thanked him reverently.

Narrator 2: The Great Spirit stood high above the valley floor and watched his chosen and he was pleased.

Great Spirit: I have brought my children to the most beautiful land in all the world and they respect the waters and trees, the earth and sky, taking only what they need and giving back to the land.

Narrator 3: The little band grew and grew and built other villages outside of Ah-wah'-nee.

Narrator 2: Together, they became the great spirit nation.

Narrator 3: One day the old Chief felt the call of the Great Spirit, so he went to his son.

Chief: My son, you will grow to be a noble Chief.

Little Lamb (Mother): But now my son, you must sleep in the skins of the beaver and the coyote, so you may be wise in building and keen of the scent of the game you hunt.

Narrator 1: As he grew older, the young Chieftain was fed trout and became a good swimmer.

Narrator 2: He ate crane eggs to grow tall and keen of sight. His favorite was the meat of the grizzly, as it made him powerful in combat.

Narrator 3: The Chieftain was wise and fair and brave. His people loved him, and they made him rich – bringing him great gifts.

Young Chieftain: Come and gather around. My gifts are your gifts. Take what you need.

Narrator 3: A group of elders met and decided the young Chieftain was to be called Choo'-too-se-ka'.

Elder 1: You are kind and generous. You have helped our grand nation to flourish.

Elder 2: You dance for the rain and respect the voices of our forefathers. From this day forward your name will be Choo'-too-se-ka'.

Narrator 1: Choo'-too-se-ka' meant Supreme Good in his language.

Narrator 2: Together with his people, they build him a grand house at the back of the great rock called To-tau-kon-nu'-la.

Narrator 3: To-tau-kon-nu'-la is called El Capitan today and legend has it that if you stand at its base, and the wind is just right, you can hear the beautiful voice of Choo'-too-se-ka' blessing his people.

Choo'-too-se-Ka': Running Bear who is that woman over there?

Running Bear: I have never seen her before. She is fair and foreign.

Narrator 3: The beautiful young woman approached them.

Tis-sa'-ack: I am Tis-sa'-ack and these are some of my people. We have come from the far south to see you and your flourishing lands, because we have heard of your great wisdom and goodness.

Tis-sa'ack's Friend: We bring you gifts of fine baskets and beads of many colors as a token of our friendship.

Choo'-too-se-Ka': You must stay and be our guests.

Tis-sa'-ack: Only until we have rested. We hope to meet your people and view your beautiful valley.

Running Bear: Come to my home and eat, then you will rest – after that consider the valley your home while you are here.

Tis-sa'-ack: Thank you very much.

Narrator 1: Choo'-too-se-ke' was so taken by his fair visitor that he built a large house for her and her companions on the summit of half dome – before it split in two.

Narrator 2: Tis-sa'-ack and her companions were happy there. They taught the women of the Ah-wah-nee to make beautiful baskets and the Chief visited her daily.

Choo'-too-se-Ka': You must stay Tis-sa'-ack. You bring beauty and happiness to our valley and its summits.

Tis-sa'-ack: You flatter me with your kind words, but the time has come for us to return home.

Choo'-too-se-Ka': Please stay and be my wife.

Tis-sa'-ack: I cannot.

Choo'-too-se-Ka': At least think about it.

Tis-sa'-ack: Your home is beautiful, and you are the most kind and gracious man I have ever met...

Choo'-too-se-Ka': Then, think about it and I will see you tomorrow.

Narrator 1: But when Choo'-too-se'-ke' arrived the next day the beautiful fair young women from the south was gone as were her companions.

Narrator 3: Legend tells us that Choo'-too-se-ke' left his people to search for her and a series of events occurred that nearly destroyed his great nation.

Narrator 2: First, there were droughts and crops failed. The rivers and streams went dry and the deer and other animals wandered away.

Narrator 1: They say a dark cloud of smoke rose in the east and blocked the sun, so it gave no heat and many of the people perished from cold and hunger.

Narrator 2: Then finally there was a great earthquake and the lovely dome, at the base of which Choo'-too-se-ke' build Tis-sa'-ack her home, split apart – half of it sliding into the valley.

Narrator 3: Then came the floods and a large part of the valley was buried in water. The Great Spirit looked down on his people and took pity.

Great Spirit: Bring new life to my chosen. Make the valley their own again.

Narrator: 1 Many moons afterwards there appeared on the face of half dome the figure of a man in a flowing robe – with one hand extended West.

Narrator 2: The figure is interpreted to be a picture of the great lost Chief and it is still looked at with awe by the descendants, of the chosen children, of the Great Spirit.

Narrator 3: If you are ever at Yosemite National Park – look to half-dome and you will see him.

Narrator 1: You will also see the face of the beautiful Tis-sa-ack on the flat side of the dome if you look closely.

Narrator 2: Or so says the legend.

The End

Why Native Americans Have So Many Tribes
Adapted from a Virginia Algonquian Legend About the Origin of the Tribes

Running Time: Six Minutes
Characters 14:

Mole 1	Mole 2	Algonquian 1	Algonquian 2	Algonquian 3
Algonquian 4	Algonquian 5	Algonquian 6	Algonquian 7	Algonquian 8
Young Algonquian		Narrator 1	Narrator 2	Narrator 3

Mole 1: I have lived so many months underground I can't stand it anymore.

Mole 2: You can't just go up there! You don't know what you'll find.

Algonquian 1: Stay with use mole. We've lived down here for so many moons - we could never count them all.

Algonquian 2: This is our home.

Algonquian 3: Our animals live in harmony with us. We are one down here and we are safe.

Mole 1: I must.

Narrator 1: With that, Mole left his family and his people and crawled up and up and up.

Narrator 2: At first, he could not open his eyes. He'd never seen the light before.

Narrator 1: But when he did...

Mole 1: Wow! It's gorgeous up here. The sky is so blue and the trees and rivers and mountains so glorious. I have to go tell the others.

Narrator 2: Mole went back to the hole and crawled down as fast as he could.

Mole 1: There is light, glorious light. And trees and rivers so clear they reflect the blue of the sky and the gray and white of the clouds.

Mole 2: But you are stumbling.

Mole 1: The light. It blinded me, but for one amazing moment I saw the world and all its wonders.

Algonquian 1: We must go for ourselves.

Algonquian 2: We have to see what Mole saw.

Algonquian 3: There is light. Light! – up here.

Narrator 2: Person after person after person climbed out of the hole.

Algonquian 4: The sky is so blue.

Algonquian 3: The trees so green and tall...

Algonquian 1: ...great giants under the glittering sun.

Algonquian 2: Oh, and what a sun! The light is like nothing else in the world.

Narrator 1: More and more people came out of the hole. One by one – until someone got stuck.

Algonquian 1: Can you hear me down there?

Algonquian 5: Yes!

Algonquian 1: Push! Push as hard as you can, and we'll pull. Come on everyone pull. Pull.

Narrator 3: As hard as they tried, they could not move the poor stuck person.

Algonquian 1: I am afraid you're stuck for good!

Algonquian 2: We must keep moving.

Narrator 2: Many of the people did not leave the darkness, but those who did, walked farther and farther.

Algonquian 3: The water is so clear and cool.

Algonquian 2: Look! A bird. What is he doing?

Narrator 1: The bird flapped its wings and parted the river.

Algonquian 1: Let's cross and see what is on the other side.

Narrator 2: Some made it across, before the waters closed again. But some could not cross.

Narrator 1: The ones who stayed were not unpleased.

Algonquian 6: We will make our home here. There is plenty to eat and drink.

Algonquian 3: It's a beautiful place to call home.

Young Algonquian: But will we ever see our friends again?

Algonquian 6: Perhaps one day, my son.

Narrator 3: The group that had passed the parted waters walked many moons until they came to rocky, high mountains.

Algonquian 1: The mountains span all the way to the sky.

Young Algonquian: Look father! A deer.

Algonquian 2: Let's follow.

Narrator 1: A large group followed the deer up and over the mountains, but soon an eagle chased the deer away.

Algonquian 7: I can no longer see the others.

Algonquian 8: We will stay here at the base of the mountains. They will protect us. There are rivers and streams and plenty of food here.

Algonquian 7: It's a beautiful place to call home.

Narrator 2: The group that passed the mountains soon found themselves in the thickest forest they'd ever seen. There were so many trees they couldn't see each other.

Narrator 3: So, they scattered – some to the north, some to the south, some to the east and some to the west.

Narrator 1: And that, according to Algonquian Legend – is why Native Americans have so many tribes.

The End

How the Deer Got His Horns
Adapted from a Cherokee Legend

Running Time: Five Minutes
Characters — 11:

Narrator 1	Narrator 2	Mother Deer	Father Deer
Father Rabbit	Mother Rabbit	Bobby	Cheeky
Chester	Young Deer	Baby Rabbit	

Narrator 1: When the moon was young, and the stars were just beginning to shine in the sky, deer had no horns.

Narrator 2: A male's head was just as smooth as that of a doe.

Narrator 1: Then, one day a mother deer and a father deer where out watching their young son run.

Narrator 2: And everything changed.

Mother Deer: Father Deer, look how fast our son runs.

Father Deer: He takes after his father.

Mother Deer: Oh you!

Narrator 1: On the other side of the tree a mother rabbit and a father rabbit were watching their young daughter hop.

Father Rabbit: Mother Rabbit, look how far our daughter can hop.

Mother Rabbit: If only she took it more seriously.

Narrator 2: Baby Rabbit was hopping and somersaulting all at the same time.

Mother Rabbit: She such a trickster.

Father Rabbit: Still, not a creature on this earth could go farther in as little time. She is the fastest furry fluff-ball in all the forest.

Mother Rabbit: And the funniest.

Narrator 1: The rabbits watched their daughter flipping and flopping and hopping all under the shade of the tall tree.

Narrator 2: Meanwhile, Bobby Bear and Cheeky Chipmunk were watching from behind a bush.

Bobby: I wonder who really could go father fastest.

Cheeky: It would be a good race. Hey Chester!

Narrator 1: Cheeky called over her brother.

Chester: Hi Bobby, hey Cheeky, what's up?

Cheeky: We want to have a race between Young Deer and Sister Rabbit to see who can go farther in the same amount of time.

Bobby: We do?

Cheeky: Isn't that what we were just talking about?

Bobby: I suppose.

Cheeky: Sure, it was.

Narrator 2: So, they called all of the animals together.

Cheeky: You don't mind do you Father Deer?

Chester: And surely you don't mind Father Rabbit?

Mother Deer and **Mother Rabbit:** What if I mind?

Father Deer: No harm in a little race. What do you say son?

Young Deer: I say, bring it.

Narrator 1: Baby Rabbit hopped into the center of the animals.

Baby Rabbit: I think it's a great idea.

Cheeky: All in fun. The two are the best of friends.

Mother Rabbit: Oh, all right.

Mother Deer: So long as it's all in fun.

Baby Rabbit: What does the winner get?

Narrator 2: Cheeky thought for a moment.

Cheeky: Chester, ' you still have that pair of antlers?

Chester: Sure do!

Cheeky: Winner gets the antlers.

Chester: Hey!

Baby Rabbit and Young Deer: I'd love to have those antlers.

Narrator 2: Everyone looked at Chester.

Narrator 1: Finally, he relented.

Chester: Oh, okay. I don't have much use for them anyway.

Narrator 1: With the race set for the next day, all of the animals went home to get a good night's sleep.

Narrator 2: On the day of the race, everyone gathered on the edge of a thick thicket.

Narrator 1: The antlers were set down to mark the starting point.

Narrator 2: While everyone was admiring the great antler horns, Baby Rabbit said:

Baby Rabbit: I don't know this part of the land very well. I think I'll just run into the bushes to see where I have to hop. You think that'd be okay?

Narrator 1: Cheeky looked at Chester and then at Bobby.

Bobby: I don't see that there'd be any harm to it. Sure, go on Baby Rabbit. Have a look.

Narrator 2: A long while passed and Baby Rabbit had not returned.

Cheeky: Maybe that wasn't such a good idea.

Chester: That Baby Rabbit can be a trickster.

Mother Rabbit: That girl. Baby Rabbit, come out of that thicket this minute.

Narrator 1: But Baby Rabbit didn't come out.

Father Rabbit: Baby Rabbit, do as you are told.

Narrator 1: Still...nothing.

Cheeky: Chester, go in and get her.

Narrator 2: Chester went into the thicket and found Baby Rabbit gnawing on the bushes.

Narrator 1: She'd gnawed so much that she'd cleared a road clean to the other side.

Narrator 2: Chester ran to tell the others.

Narrator 1: When Baby Rabbit came out...

Cheeky: Baby Rabbit you tried to cheat.

Baby Rabbit: I did not.

Chester: You did so, you cleared a road. I saw it.

Baby Rabbit: I did not.

Chester: Have a look for yourselves.

Narrator 2: All of the animals followed Chester into the thicket.

Narrator 1: And they saw the road.

Father Rabbit: Baby Rabbit. You should be ashamed of yourself.

Mother Rabbit: Looks like Young Deer gets the antlers.

Narrator 2: They all agreed.

Narrator 1: And that is why, to this day, deer wear antlers.

Narrator 2: That's also why, to this day, rabbits go around gnawing on bushes.

The End

The Legend of the No-Face Doll

Adapted from the Haudenosaunee, or Six Nations, People

Running Time: Six Minutes

Characters - 15:

Narrator 1	Narrator 2	Narrator 3	Wind
Beans Spirit	Squash Spirit	Corn Spirit	Villager 1
Girl Villager	Next Villager 1	Next Villager Girl 1	Next Villager Girl 2
Last Villager 1	Great Spirit	Haudenosaunee Girl	

Each actor is to say his or her name and the character they play before the play begins.

Narrator 1: Early colonists called the Haudenosaunee the Iroquois Confederacy, so that's probably how you know them, but really, they are the Haudenosaunee or Six Nations.

Narrator 2: The Haudenosaunee, or Six Nations, are made up of six tribes: the Mohawk, Seneca, Oneida, Onondaga, Cayuga and Tuscarora.

Narrator 3: To this day, they do not put faces on their dolls. This is why:

Haudenosaunee Girl 1: Since ancient times, my people have respected the Three Sisters: Corn, Beans and Squash. One day the Great Spirit called them to come before it.

Great Spirit: Oh, Wind that washes the air clean – bring to me the Three Sisters: Core, Beans and Squash.

Wind: As you command Great Spirit.

Narrator 1: Wind whooshed away and returned with the Three Sisters on its tail.

Great Spirit: I have called you Three Sisters to anoint you the Sustainers of Life.

78

Beans Spirit: I am humbled Great Spirit.

Narrator 1: Squash knelt before the Great Spirit.

Squash Spirit: I will serve with honor.

Beans Spirit: As will I.

Corn Spirit: Great Spirit, the honor is so grand, we will serve and sustain all of the people of the Six Nations, but surely there is something more I can do for my people.

Great Spirit: Corn Spirit, take from yourself and craft a doll from your husk.

Corn Spirit: Thank you.

Narrator 2: The Great Spirit left the sisters.

Narrator 3: And the Corn Spirit went to work on her doll.

Beans Spirit: It is beautiful sister.

Squash Spirit: It is the most beautiful doll I've ever seen.

Beans Spirit: The face is perfect. You must make more.

Corn Spirit: Thank you, but we can't neglect our duties.

Narrator 1: The Corn Spirit looked at her doll and smiled.

Corn Spirit: It is the most beautiful face I have ever seen.

Narrator 2: Corn took the doll from village to village for the children to play with.

Villager 1: The doll is so beautiful.

Villager Girl 1: Thank you for sharing her with us – if only for a bit.

Narrator 3: The reaction from village to village was the same.

Next Villager 1: Be careful with her daughter. Corn you sustain us and now you honor use by allowing our children to play with your doll.

Next Villager Girl 1: She is wonderful.

Next Villager Girl 2: Her face is perfect.

Corn Spirit: Thank you for allowing me to serve and sustain you.

Narrator 2: It wasn't long before all of the compliments started to go to Corn's head.

Narrator 3: And Corn Spirit grew conceited.

Last Villager 1: She is the most beautiful doll I have seen.

Corn Spirit: I know. I crafted her face to look like mine.

Narrator 1: Corn Spirit took her doll back. A group of children asked if they could see the doll one more time.

Corn Spirit: You have had your chance. I am in demand. I must go to the next village, so they can have a glimpse of my beautiful doll.

Narrator 2: Beans Spirit and Squash Spirit joined their sister as she traveled to the next village.

Squash Spirit: Corn, we have been watching as you travel.

Beans Spirit: And you are changing. Do not let your good work and beauty go to your head.

Corn Spirit: Sisters, you do not understand how popular I am.

Narrator 3: The Great Spirit was displeased.

Great Spirit: Wind, bring Corn Spirit to me.

Narrator 1: Wind whooshed through the sky and said to Corn Spirit.

Wind: The Great Spirit has summoned you.

Narrator 2: Corn Spirit started off with Wind to the lodge of the Great Spirit.

Narrator 3: On her way, she saw a calm, clear pool of water and stopped to admire herself.

Narrator 1: When Corn Spirit arrived at the Great Spirit's lodge she could tell he was not pleased.

Great Spirit: Corn Spirit I am disappointed.

Corn Spirit: I am so sorry.

Great Spirit: If you keep thinking you are better than everyone - a tremendous punishment will come to you.

Corn Spirit: I apologize Great Spirit, but what will happen? What will become of me? What will the punishment be?

Great Spirit: You do not want to know.

Narrator 2: Corn Spirit continued from village to village.

Narrator 3: And again, everyone kept telling her how beautiful she was and how wonderful her doll was.

Narrator 1: It wasn't long before Corn Spirit grew conceited again.

Great Spirit: I have warned you.

Narrator 2: As Corn Spirit passed another clear pool of water, she stopped to admire herself.

Corn Spirit: No!

Narrator 3: When she looked in the pool, she did not have a face.

Narrator 1: It was taken by the Great Spirit.

Narrator 2: Since that ancient time, the Haudenosaunee people do not put faces on their corn husk dolls.

Narrator 3: This is to remind them never to think they are better than anyone else.

Narrator 1: Or a great punishment will fall upon them.

The End

THE CORN SPIRIT READERS THEATER
Based on a Tuscarora Harvest Legend

CHARACTERS 11:

NARRATOR 1	NARRATOR 2	GIRL 1	GIRL2
FATHER	MOTHER	AUNT	SON 1
SON 2	DAYOHAGWENDA	OLD MAN	

NARRATOR 1: Long ago, the ancestors of the Tuscarora were blessed with good harvests year after year.

NARRATOR 2: Corn was plentiful, and the people began to take it for granted.

GIRL 1: It's time to go to the corn fields and bring in the rest of the crops.

GIRL 2: I'm tired today.

GIRL 3: Don't you think we have enough? Father what do you think?

GIRL 1: I'm beginning to not like autumn at all.

FATHER: Daughters, you work hard. Rest today and tomorrow we'll inspect the fields together.

MOTHER: It's time for breakfast. Come and eat.

NARRATOR 1: When mother set the food out for her family, they ate very little.

GIRL 2: I'm too full to finish.

GIRL 1: Me too.

FATHER: Give the rest to the dogs.

NARRATOR 1: Mother shook her head but said nothing.

NARRATOR 2: After breakfast she went to help her sister prepare the corn for winter.

MOTHER: I fear for my family, for all of our people.

AUNT: That's a strange thing to say. What do even mean?

MOTHER: We waste so much. We throw away our food, we leave crops in the field.

AUNT: You worry too much. We've plenty. Our stores of corn are substantial, and the forests are full of game, large and small.

NARRATOR 1: That afternoon, Father went with his sons to hunt.

SON 1: Father, Father I got it.

FATHER: And what a catch.

SON 1: And with a single, solitary shot.

SON 2: Brother, that's the biggest deer I've ever seen.

SON 1: The forest is full of deer and rabbits. We'll eat forever.

NARRATOR 2: The next morning father went with his daughters to walk the fields.

FATHER: There's so much left.

GIRL 3: But we have so much.

GIRL 1: Plus, if we run out of corn, the forests are rich with game.

GIRL 2: You said so yourself.

FATHER: Let's go watch the boys play Lacrosse.

NARRATOR 1: The whole village gathered to watch a pick-up Lacrosse match.

NARRATOR 2: They left most of the corn in the fields for the birds to eat.

NARRATOR 1: Except for Dayohagwenda.

NARRATOR 2: Father noticed he was not at the match.

NARRATOR 1: During a break in the match, Father went to Dayohagwenda's home to see if he was okay.

NARRATOR 2: But Dayohagwenda and his family weren't there.

MOTHER: Check his fields.

SON 1: They have plenty of stored corn – why would they be in the fields?

SON 2: I'll come with you. We're losing because Little Eagle's not here.

NARRATOR 1: So, father went to Dayohagwenda's fields.

NARRATOR 2: There he found the entire family carefully harvesting the corn.

FATHER: Dayohagwenda, we missed you at the match today.

DAYOHAGWENDA: We have work to do.

FATHER: You have plenty. We are blessed, year after year, with great crops and plenty of game.

DAYOHAGWENDA: I'm sad for you, for the entire community. When was the last time you thanked the Creator for your good fortune?

FATHER: After the match.

NARRATOR 1: They left Dayohagwenda and his family.

DAYOHAGWENDA: Thank you Creator for our abundance.

LITTLE EAGLE: And I thank you Creator for the abundance of our whole community.

NARRATOR 1: Dayohagwenda, looked at his son and smiled.

NARRATOR 2: Proud of how the young boy acted.

NARRATOR 1: Autumn came, and the men went to the forest to hunt.

NARRATOR 2: But the deer, the moose and even the rabbits had all but vanished.

NARRATOR 1: They went first to the lakes and then to the streams.

NARRATOR 2: But there wasn't a fish to be found.

MOTHER: Father, the corn…it's gone.

FATHER: Gone? What do you mean gone?

GIRL 1: The baskets have rotted away.

GIRL 2: And the ones that're left are filled with mice.

GIRL 3: We'll starve.

SON 1: What are we going to do, Father?

NARRATOR 1: Meanwhile, Dayohagwenda was walking in the forest.

DAYOHAGWENDA: Creator, I fear for my people who no longer give you thanks.

NARRATOR 2: Dayohagwenda found an old trail.

NARRATOR 1: It led to a clearing in the forest.

NARRATOR 2: There he found an old lodge, made of elm bark, built high on top of a mound of earth.

NARRATOR 1: Weeds grew around the lodge and an old man, in tattered clothes, sat with tears in his eyes.

NARRATOR 2: Dayohagwenda was curious. He thought he knew everyone in this part of the forest.

NARRATOR 1: But he'd never seen this old man before.

DAYOHAGWENDA: Sir, why are you crying?

OLD MAN: Because your people have forgotten me.

DAYOHAGWENDA: And your clothes? Why are they torn?

OLD MAN: They're torn because your people threw me to their dogs.

DAYOHAGWENDA: But why are you dirty?

OLD MAN: I am dirty because your people let their children trample all over me.

DAYOHAGWENDA: The weeds, sir, why are their weeds all around your lodge?

OLD MAN: They are there because your people no longer take care of me.

NARRATOR 2: Then it hit Dayohagwenda.

NARRATOR 1: He knew who the old man was.

DAYOHAGWENDA: Sir, respectfully I ask, are you the Corn Spirit?

NARRATOR 2: A tear fell from the old man's face and dropped to the dry earth.

OLD MAN: Now I must go away and never return to help them again.

DAYOHAGWENDA: Please don't leave us.

OLD MAN: I have no choice. Your people have forsaken me.

DAYOHAGWENDA: Give me one more chance. Let me go back and remind my people how to treat you.

NARRATOR 1: The Corn Spirit looked at him for a long time.

NARRATOR 2: Finally, he spoke.

OLD MAN: I will stay if your people show me respect.

NARRATOR 2: Dayohagwenda ran back to his village.

DAYOHAGWENDA: Little Eagle, take your brothers and gather the people.

NARRATOR1: In no time, all of his people stood in front of his home.

AUNT: All of the corn is gone!

FATHER: And the forest is barren.

SON 1: The deer and the moose...

SON 2: ...and even the rabbits have disappeared.

DAYOHAGWENDA: I was walking in the forest and I stumbled across a lodge. It was surrounded by weeds and in front of it sat an old man in clothing, the color of corn husks, only it was tattered and torn.

FATHER: It was the Corn Spirit.

NARRATOR 2: Dayohagwenda nodded.

DAYOHAGWENDA: And he said he would leave us because his people have deserted him.

MOTHER: We have been fools.

AUNT: Horrible, horrible fools.

GIRL 1: Without food, we'll die.

GIRL 2: I'm so ashamed.

FATHER: Dayohagwenda, isn't there anything we can do?

DAYOHAGWENDA: We have a chance. I spoke with him and told him we would treat him with respect.

GIRL 3: What did he say?

DAYOHAGWENDA: He said, if we respect him he'll help us through the wind.

NARRATOR 1: Dayohagwenda dug up his own stores of corn.

NARRATOR 2: His wife and daughters took care to make their baskets well.

NARRATOR 1: When he saw his baskets full of corn, he was confused. He looked at his son.

DAYOHAGWENDA: Little Eagle, we didn't have this much corn before.

LITTLE EAGLE: You're right. There's more here than we harvested.

DAYOHAGWENDA: There's enough for the entire village to last through the winter.

NARRATOR 1: Both father and son took a moment to thank the Corn Spirit.

NARRATOR 2: The rest of the did the same.

NARRATOR 1: The next season, all of his people planted with care.

NARRATOR 2: And they tended their fields and gave thanks to the Corn Spirit.

NARRATOR 1: And when harvest came, they sang their thanksgiving.

NARRATOR 2: They taught their children and their children's children, on down the line, to do the same.

NARRATOR 1: And, so, it is to this day.

THE END

References

Orrin Lewis "Native American Indian Legends and Folklore." http://www.native-languages.org/languages.htm. Web. September 2018.

Miwok Yosemite: http://www.sacred-texts.com/nam/ca/lly/lly26.htm
How the Deer Got His Horns: http://www.sacred-texts.com/nam/cher/motc/motc026.htm

Cherokee Children information from Manataka American Indian Council
https://www.manataka.org/page1969.html

Powhatan census reference: Egloff, Keith and Deborah Woodward. *First People: The Early Indians of Virginia*, Charlottesville, VA: University Press of Virginia, 1992

Six Nations: "Six Nations of the Iroquois." https://www.britannica.com/list/the-6-nations-of-the-iroquois-confederacy. Web. September 2018

Tuscarora. http://www.newworldencyclopedia.org/entry/Tuscarora_(tribe). Web. September 2018.

"Reading Fluency Chart" information pulled from "Hasbrouck & Tindal (2006):
http://www.brtprojects.org/wp-content/uploads/2016/05/TechRpt33_FluencyNorms.pdf
(September 21, 2018) and The Reading Teacher in 2006 (Hasbrouck, J. & Tindal, G. A. (2006). Oral reading fluency norms: A valuable assessment tool for reading teachers.

Online teacher resources:
- Powhatan: http://www.native-languages.org/powhatan.htm
- Native American Facts for Kids: http://www.native-languages.org/kids.htm
- Native American Heritage: https://www.scholastic.com/teachers/collections/teaching-content/native-american-heritage-0/

Photo Credits

Answers

Page 13:   "The Theft of Fire" – Version 1: Comprehension Assessment
   1. d; 2.b; 3.c; 4.c; 5.d; 6.d

Page 18:   "The Theft of Fire" – Version 2: Comprehension Assessment
   1. b; 2.b; 3.c; 4.a; 5.a; 6.c

Page 24:   "Legend of Choo-too-se-ke' and Tis-sa'-sak" Comprehension Assessment
   1. b; 2.a; 3.c; 4.a; 5.b; 6.d

Page 30:   "Why Native American's Have So Many Tribes" Comprehension Assessment
   1. d; 2.c; 3.d; 4.a; 5.d; 6.b

Page 34   Cherokee Children: 1. a; 2.a

Page 36   "How the Deer Got His Horns" Comprehension Assessment
   1. c; 2.a; 3.d; 4.b; 5.a; 6. answers will vary

Page 41:   Six Nations: 1. c; 2.d

Page 43:   "The Legend of the No-Face Doll" Comprehension Assessment
   1. b; 2.a; 3.c; 4.a; 5.b; 6.b

Page 50:   "The Corn Spirit Reader's Theater" Comprehension Assessment
   1. b; 2.d; 3.a; 4.c 5. answers will vary

Page 51:   Tuscarora Culture and History Warm-Up: 1.a;2.b;3.b;4c

www.ingramcontent.com/pod-product-compliance
Lightning Source LLC
LaVergne TN
LVHW061336060426

835511LV00014B/1949